D1281507

Buddy BOOKS
Prehistoric Animals

Woolly Rhinoceros

ABDO
Publishing Company

A Buddy Book
by
Michael P. Goecke

VISIT US AT
www.abdopub.com

Published by Buddy Books, an imprint of ABDO Publishing Company, 4940 Viking Drive, Edina, Minnesota 55435. Copyright © 2004 by Abdo Consulting Group, Inc. International copyrights reserved in all countries. No part of this book may be reproduced in any form without written permission from the publisher.

Printed in the United States.

Edited by: Christy DeVillier
Contributing Editor: Matt Ray
Graphic Design: Deborah Coldiron
Image Research: Deborah Coldiron
Illustrations: Deborah Coldiron, Denise Esner
Photographs: Corel, Steve McHugh, Minden Pictures

Library of Congress Cataloging-in-Publication Data

Goecke, Michael P., 1968-
    Woolly rhinoceros / Michael P. Goecke.
       p. cm. — (Prehistoric animals. Set II)
    Includes bibliographical references and index.
    Summary: Introduces the physical characteristics, habitat, and behavior of the prehistoric relative of modern-day rhinos.
    ISBN 1-57765-978-3
    1. Woolly rhinoceros—Juvenile literature. [1. Woolly rhinoceros. 2. Rhinoceroses, Fossil. 3. Prehistoric animals. 4. Paleontology.] I. Title.

QE882.U6 .G26 2003
569'.668—dc21

                                                            2002032279

Table of Contents

Prehistoric Animals

Many exciting animals lived in **prehistoric** times. There were saber-toothed cats, woolly mammoths, and many others. Scientists study **fossils** to learn about prehistoric animals. Fossils help them understand the prehistoric world.

Dinosaurs are famous prehistoric animals.

Prehistoric Animals

The Woolly Rhinoceros

Woolly Rhinoceros
(WUH-lee ry-NOS-ruhs)

The woolly rhinoceros lived in **prehistoric** times. It is famous for its horns and hairy coat.

Scientists have names for important time periods in Earth's history. The woolly rhinoceros lived during a time period called the Pleistocene. The Pleistocene began about two million years ago.

A Geologic Timeline
248 Million Years Ago – Today

Triassic	Jurassic	Cretaceous	Paleocene	Eocene	Oligocene	Miocene	Pliocene	Pleistocene	Holocene
248 – 213 Million Years Ago	213 – 145 Million Years Ago	145 – 65 Million Years Ago	65 – 56 Million Years Ago	56 – 34 Million Years Ago	34 – 24 Million Years Ago	24 – 5 Million Years Ago	5 – 2 Million Years Ago	2 Million – 11,500 Years Ago	11,500 Years Ago – Today

Age Of Dinosaurs	**Age Of Mammals**
248 – 65 Million Years Ago	65 Million Years Ago – Today

The woolly rhinoceros lived between 500,000 and 10,000 years ago.

The woolly rhinoceros was as big as some of today's rhinos. Adult males grew to become about six feet (two m) tall. Some woolly rhinoceroses were 11 feet (3 m) long. Females were smaller.

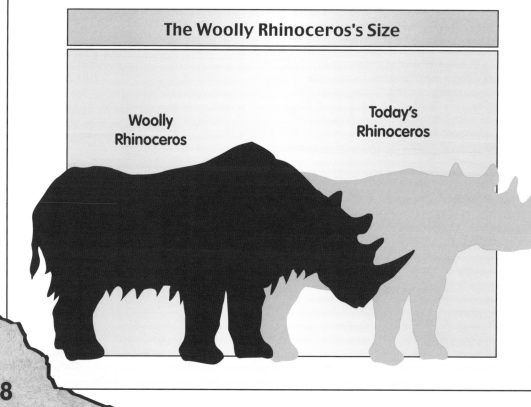

The Woolly Rhinoceros's Size

Woolly Rhinoceros

Today's Rhinoceros

Unlike rhinos today, the woolly rhinoceros was very hairy. It had a thick coat of shaggy hair. The hair was probably grayish brown.

The woolly rhinoceros had short legs and small ears. It had two horns on its nose. The longer horn was not round. It had flat sides like a wooden board. This longer horn could grow to be almost five feet (two m) long.

Fun Facts

Sumatran Rhinos

The Sumatran rhino is related to the woolly rhinoceros. It has been around for millions of years.

The Sumatran rhino lives in Asia. Like the woolly rhinoceros, it has two horns. The Sumatran rhino eats fruits, leaves, and shrubs. It eats at night.

A Sumatran rhino.

There are not many Sumatran rhinos left in the world. Hunting Sumatran rhinos is against the law. But people do it anyway. Scientists fear that Sumatran rhinos will soon become extinct.

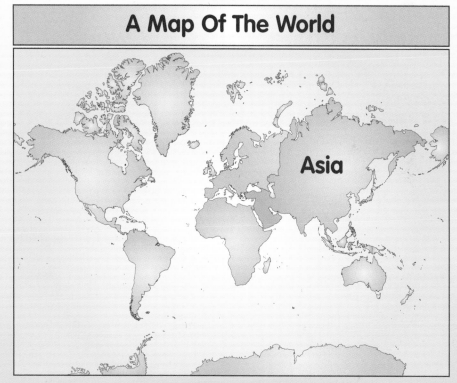

A Map Of The World

Asia

Sumatran rhinos live in Asia.

Today's rhinos mostly live alone or in small family groups. The woolly rhinoceros probably lived this way, too.

Like rhinos today, the woolly rhinoceros ate plants. It probably ate grasses, mosses, and lichens.

Scientists believe the woolly rhinoceros cleared away snow with its bigger horn. This would help it find grass to eat.

The woolly rhinoceros ate grass and other plants.

13

Predators

Most predators do not hunt big animals like rhinos. The only hunters of today's rhinos are people. Prehistoric people may have killed woolly rhinoceroses, too.

Prehistoric people lived in caves. They painted on cave walls. Some of these cave paintings show the woolly rhinoceros. Some scientists believe prehistoric people trapped woolly rhinoceroses in pits.

15

Cave paintings by prehistoric people
are still around today.

The woolly rhinoceros was around for thousands of years. It lived during the last Ice Age. During the Ice Age, the world became cooler. Giant sheets of ice covered many lands. The woolly rhinoceros's thick coat kept it warm.

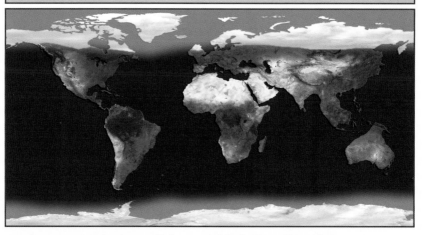

The Pleistocene World

Ice covered parts of the world during the Pleistocene.

The woolly rhinoceros lived in Asia and Europe. It lived on grass steppes. This land had mixed grasses and few trees. Woolly mammoths and saber-toothed cats may have lived there, too.

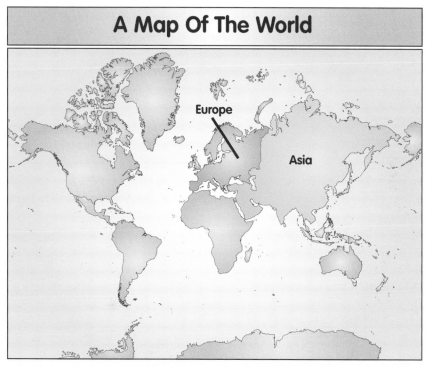

A Map Of The World

Europe

Asia

Woolly rhinoceros fossils have been found in Asia and Europe.

The woolly rhinoceros probably lived among
saber-toothed cats.

The woolly rhinoceros became extinct about 10,000 years ago. No one is sure why this happened. Maybe an illness killed it. A climate change may have killed the plants it ate. Maybe prehistoric people hunted them to death. Scientists hope to solve this mystery one day.

In the 1800s, people in Russia found many woolly rhinoceros horns. They did not know what these fossils were. Some people thought the horns were claws from a giant bird.

Horns from some woolly rhinoceroses are around today as fossils.

People found woolly rhinoceros skulls, too. These skulls still had horns. Long ago, people thought these bones belonged to dragons or unicorns. Today, people know that dragons and unicorns are not real.

Unicorns are make-believe animals.

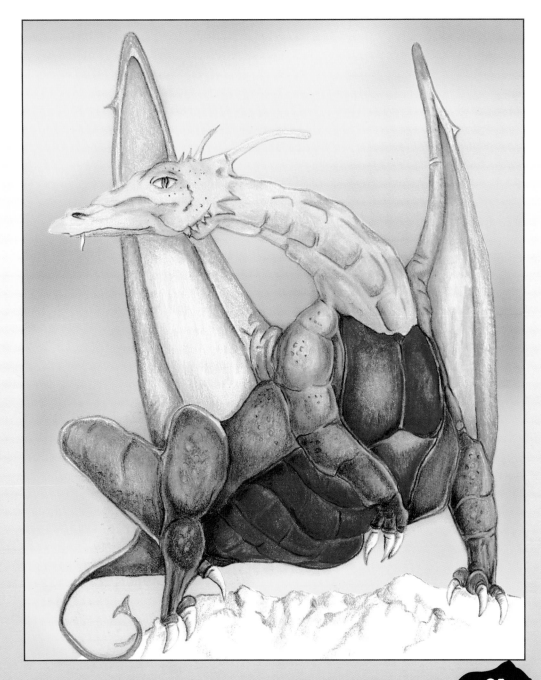

Dragons are not real.

This boy is holding a woolly rhinoceros fossil.

Many woolly rhinoceros fossils have been found in Europe and Asia. Some of them were whole animals. These fossils were frozen in ice or buried underground. Fossils help people understand what the woolly rhinoceros was like.

Important Words

climate the weather of a place over time.

extinct when all members of a species no longer exist, or live.

fossil remains of very old animals and plants commonly found in the ground. A fossil can be a bone, a footprint, or any trace of life.

Ice Age a period in Earth's history when ice covered parts of the world. The last Ice Age ended about 11,500 years ago.

lichens plants without flowers, leaves, or roots.

predator an animal that hunts and eats other animals.

prehistoric describes anything that was around more than 5,500 years ago.

Web Sites

To learn more about the woolly rhinoceros, visit ABDO Publishing Company on the World Wide Web. Web sites about the woolly rhinoceros are featured on our Book Links page. These links are routinely monitored and updated to provide the most current information available.

www.abdopub.com

Index

24